THE SAD NIGHT

THE SAD NIGHT

The Story of an Aztec Victory and a Spanish Loss

WRITTEN AND ILLUSTRATED BY

SALLY SCHOFER MATHEWS

CLARION BOOKS NEW YORK

This book is for the Schofer family
and memories of Mexico.

Clarion Books
a Houghton Mifflin Company imprint
16645
215 Park Avenue South, New York, NY 10003
Text and illustrations copyright © 1994 by Sally Schofer Mathews
Illustrations executed in black ink and watercolors.
Text set in 13 point Galliard.

Design by Sally Schofer Mathews and Sylvia Frezzolini
Printed in the USA

Library of Congress Cataloging-in-Publication Data
Mathews, Sally Schofer.
The Sad Night: the story of an Aztec victory and a Spanish
loss / written and illustrated by Sally Schofer Mathews.   p.   cm.
Summary: Tells how the Aztecs established an empire in Mexico and
what happened when they, led by Montezuma, encountered Cortés
and the Spaniards in the early sixteenth century.
    ISBN 0-395-63035-5
1. Mexico—History—Conquest, 1519-1540—Juvenile literature.
2. Aztecs—Wars—Juvenile literatures. [1 Mexico—History—
Conquest, 1519-1540. 2. Aztecs. Aztecs—History. 3. Indians of
Mexico—History.] I. Title.   F1230.M392   1993
                                   972.02—dc20   92—25119 CIP
                                                               AC
HOR   10 9 8 7 6 5 4 3 2 1 *3. Aztecs-History*

The Aztecs and other peoples of Mexico wrote with pictures on bark pages that were connected together in one long accordion-folded piece. We call these "books" codices.

Five hundred years ago, when Spanish soldiers conquered Mexico, they collected and destroyed almost all the codices. The artwork of this true story is based on the fewer than twenty codices and codex fragments that remain.

Three words from the Aztec language, Nahuatl (NAH hwatl), are pictured and pronounced below.

Tenochtitlán
teh notch teet LAHN

Moctezuma
mock teh ZOO ma

Quetzalcoatl
ket sahl KWAHtl

Long ago in Mexico, when volcanoes sent lava rivers steaming into the jungles and jaguars hissed messages to man, a wandering people listened to their leaders.

"We must move again," the priests said. "Put on your sandals and your robes and take your children by the hand, and walk and keep on walking until you see an eagle on a cactus with a rattlesnake in its beak. In that place, we will build an empire."

Every day they walked. To sleep, they curled up in their robes. To eat, they chopped up cactus and roasted rattlesnake meat. And one day, one very good day, they looked across a lake and saw an eagle on an island. It was perched on a cactus, with a rattlesnake twisting around in its beak. They named the island Tenochtitlán, which means "the place of the cactus stone."

"We must make boats," the leaders said, "to get from here to the island, and when we live there, we'll travel on streets of water. And we must make our buildings tall enough to meet the sun, for the sun will light the way for us to become a noble people."

The people worked hard. They built huge stone pyramids and put temples on top. They constructed palaces of stone with hundreds of rooms. They built causeways across the lake with bridges they could take away. They were safe. They were strong. They were the Aztecs.

They began to want their neighbors' land. Ferocious Aztec warriors, the Jaguar Knights and the Eagle Knights, took over territory

that belonged to other Indians and forced them to pay again and again to stay alive.

The Aztecs had built an empire in less than two hundred years. Everyone was afraid of them, and their king, Moctezuma, was the most powerful man in Mexico.

Trouble for the Aztecs began in the year of 1-Reed, 1519. The king's men reminded him of the warning. "Danger will come to us this year by boat, Royal Moctezuma. Our ancestors told us that the Feathered Serpent god would return to Mexico to take over our kingdom. They said that when he comes, Quetzalcoatl will not look like a feathered serpent, but like a man.

"If he takes over, what will become of us? Are we doomed? Royal prince, what should we do?"

"Quetzalcoatl is not a god of war," said Moctezuma. "He wants poems and beauty and thoughtful, thoughtful words. Perhaps he comes to test us. I will wait, I will see, and then I will decide. For now, we will wait, and I will make an offering to the god."

Hidden by the jungle, Aztec lookouts watched the biggest boats they had ever seen anchor on their shores. Soldiers wearing metal clothes crawled from the ships, then burned and sank the ships. The lookouts ran back over the mountains to Tenochtitlán with the news: Quetzalcoatl and his army had arrived from the direction of the sunrise.

But it was not Quetzalcoatl who had arrived on the eastern shore of Mexico. It was Hernán Cortés, a captain from Spain, sailing along the coast in search of gold and land. He and his small army had met some Indians who were friendly and some who had tried to chase them away. All were unhappy with the harsh Aztec rule.

Moctezuma sent messengers to the Spanish campsite with golden

gifts for Quetzalcoatl. He hoped the god would bless the Aztecs, then go back home. But Cortés, realizing he had been mistaken for a god, began the long march to Tenochtitlán.

Again Moctezuma chose important gifts from his treasury of gold and jewels, and he and his men met Cortés and his army on a causeway.

Does a king fight a god? Only if he wants to die. Moctezuma welcomed Cortés. "Please consider my palaces your home. Come rest and eat. We are ready for you."

The Spanish soldiers stared in amazement at the beauty of Tenochtitlán, and the noble Moctezuma, and their golden presents. They asked one another, "Are we in heaven?"

Yet in the palace the soldiers of Spain went to bed with their boots on, in full armor, clutching their weapons. Outside, the Aztec warriors whispered to each other that gods or not, the Spaniards seemed like enemies. On their march from the coast, Cortés and his army had killed many Indians with weapons no one had seen before: cannons, guns, metal knives, dogs trained to attack, and horses that carried soldiers.

The Aztec generals wanted Spanish blood to flow. "Say the word, Royal Moctezuma," they snarled, "and before the sun leaves us today, we will slay these intruders as quickly as a jaguar pounces on a rabbit."

Meanwhile, the Spanish soldiers complained to Cortés. "There are

thousands of Aztec warriors and only four hundred of us. You must do something to protect us, sir. Please do it now."

So Cortés, his captains, and Doña Marina, their Indian interpreter, marched to the royal palace. With strong, smooth words, they asked Moctezuma to come stay with them as a hostage until they felt safe. Moctezuma did not want to go. "You are my guests," he assured them. "Therefore you cannot be in danger."

Afraid that their plan might fail, a Spanish soldier threatened to stab him. To prevent bloodshed, Doña Marina urged Moctezuma to go with them quickly. The king agreed, ordered his guards not to move, and went with Cortés.

Though Moctezuma was still in command of Mexico, he was a prisoner. He turned over to Cortés all the gold in his treasury room. The Spaniards melted the gold and gold jewelry into bars small enough to carry in their clothes.

Moctezuma's advisors visited him often and tried to persuade him to leave. "We can overpower them," they insisted.

The king refused. "I will wait," he said. "I will not fight Quetzalcoatl. I will not fight a god."

Aztec lookouts from the eastern coast ran to Moctezuma with an

important message: nineteen more Spanish ships had landed at Vera Cruz. Moctezuma told Cortés that more Spaniards had arrived, expecting him to be pleased. But Cortés knew the newcomers were not his friends. The king of Spain had sent troops to capture him, since he had burned his ships and acted on his own.

Commanding an officer named Pedro de Alvarado to keep control in Tenochtitlán, Cortés took some troops and left on horseback for Vera Cruz. He planned to defeat the new arrivals and then talk them into joining him in the search for more gold.

Meanwhile, Alvarado gave the Aztecs permission to dance in a religious ceremony in front of the Great Temple. A huge crowd gathered, and Alvarado and his men, fearing an uprising, struck first. They slaughtered every priest, musician, and dancer in the courtyard.

Moctezuma, shocked and angry but still a prisoner, commanded his army to hold back. "Wait until their leader returns," he said. "I believe he will punish his soldiers for this act of war. You will see."

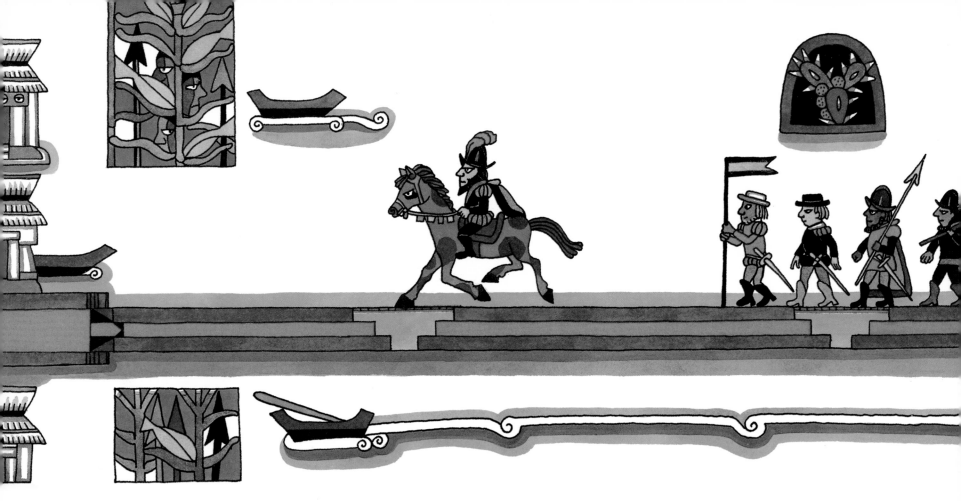

When Cortés returned, followed by an army of several thousand soldiers, he rode his horse along a deserted causeway. No procession came to greet him, no Aztec lords with gifts of gold. The heavy marching of his soldiers echoed down the streets.

In the palace, Cortés raged at Alvarado for the slaughter. But there would be no pardon, for the Aztec warriors, outnumbering the Spaniards by thousands, swarmed over the rooftops and filled the streets, slinging rocks and attacking with clubs, arrows, spears, and fire.

"Take Moctezuma to the roof," Cortés ordered, "and make him tell his people to stop. Tell them we'll leave peacefully."

Turning his face from the Spaniards, Moctezuma said quietly, "I welcomed you as a god returning to his own land, yet you are destroying us. My people are angry. They have chosen another to be

king when I die, and they have made up their minds not to let you leave this place alive. I can no longer help you."

Nevertheless, he tried to end the fighting by climbing to the roof to speak to his people. He told them that if they stopped their attack, the Spaniards would leave Mexico.

An angry person in the crowd threw some stones at Moctezuma. Suddenly many people were throwing stones, and Moctezuma fell. The Spaniards laid him on a mat, but he refused their doctor's help. In a cell of his family palace, the king of the Aztec sun died in pain and sorrow.

By custom, Aztec warriors did not fight at night. They removed the bridges from the causeways, so no one could enter or leave the city, and went home to sleep. The Spanish soldiers secretly had been building a portable wooden span to use as a bridge.

Night came, and the Aztecs left the palace courtyards and deserted the streets. Rainfall darkened the sky and would muffle the sound of

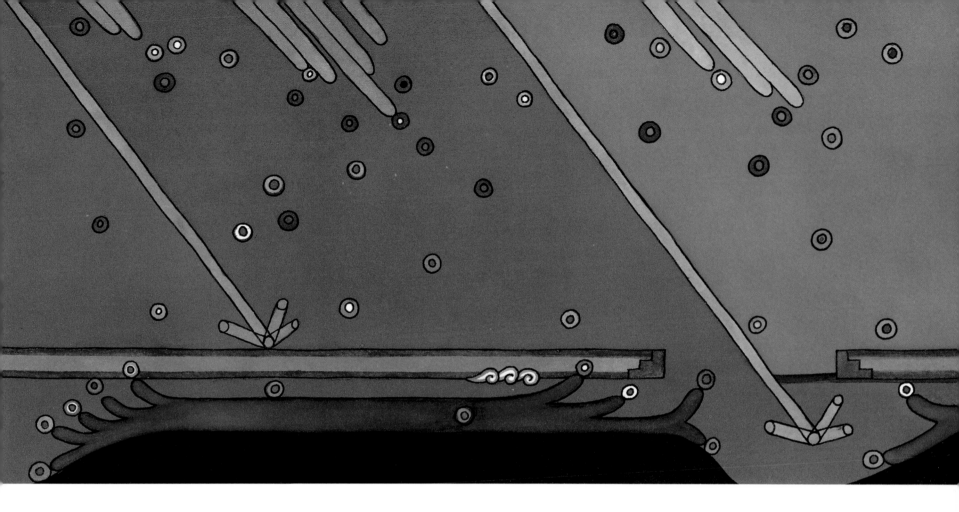

marching. The Spaniards took this chance to escape, knowing they might not get another. They loaded some of the Aztec gold onto horses and helped themselves to the rest of it. Carrying heavy weapons and weighted down with gold, the men moved quickly toward the causeway. At a gate an Aztec sentry saw them and shouted an alarm.

At the first gap in the causeway the Spaniards lowered their wooden bridge. It held strong as the parade of soldiers, horses, and cannons crowded across.

But Aztecs were behind them, running toward them from the city. They were sliding through the water in hundreds of canoes. Yelling for room to work, the Spanish crews pulled and tugged at the bridge to lift it up, but it was stuck.

Aztecs were bumping their canoes into the side of the causeway, climbing out, and jumping onto the bridge. Thousands of warriors attacked the Spaniards and pushed them forward.

Those Spaniards at the front of the line shouted for the soldiers to bring up the bridge, but the men at the end of the line were fighting and shoving and pushing and pulling.

In the bitter struggle, both Aztecs and Spaniards fell off the edge of the causeway into the water, but the Aztecs were not weighted down with gold and could swim.

So many men died and sank into the water where the bridge should have been that the last Spaniards crossed over the gap on drowned bodies. The Aztecs did not follow them to shore. They took the Spanish wounded and captured to sacrifice to their gods.

Near the bloodied causeway, Cortés sat in the rain under a cypress tree and wept. He had lost most of his men and his horses and the gold. Spaniards who wrote down the story of that night and Spain's terrible losses called the escape from Tenochtitlán *The Sad Night*.

But many Aztec Eagle Knights and many Jaguar Knights also died that night. The Aztecs did not know that this was the last battle they would win.

A year later, Cortés and his men marched back with more cannons and more men. With the help of the Tlascalan people, they had built a small fleet of ships which were then taken apart and carried piece by piece over the mountains. The ships were reassembled at the lakeshore. This time the Spaniards fought the Aztecs to the ground and conquered the city.

The ancient stone pyramids and temples were torn down. Spaniards forced Aztec slaves to build churches and public buildings on top of the ruins, using the same stones.

Some of those buildings are still there today. Tenochtitlán is now Mexico City, the largest city in the world. It is no longer an island; the lakes and streets of water have dried up.

A few years ago, workers digging in the city for a new subway found three bars of gold. Experts studied them and saw traces of melted-down jewelry from Moctezuma's treasure that was lost in the lake.

Almost five hundred years after The Sad Night, the president of Mexico and the ambassador from Spain met as friends in a great museum

in Mexico City to inspect the gold bars. Over that building in the heart of the city waves the flag of Mexico. The people who give their allegiance to this flag speak Spanish, the language of Cortés, yet on that flag is this design: an eagle perched on a cactus on a rock with a snake in its beak.

Quetzalcoatl

Moctezuma II

MORE ABOUT
THE AZTECS AND CORTÉS

Hernán Cortés

Doña Marina

Tenochtitlán was founded around 1345. By 1519 it had grown into a city larger than any in Europe.

Three great causeways connected the island to the mainland. A few large roadways criss-crossed the city, but most of the 200,000 inhabitants traveled by boat through a maze-like network of canals.

Many of the city's 60,000 homes were built on *chinampas* (chee-NAM-pas), garden areas in the lake formed from layers of matted vegetation and mud, anchored at the edges with willow trees.

In the main plaza two sacred chapels atop a huge pyramid base formed the Great Temple

to the rain and war gods, shown above. Nearby was the round temple of Quetzalcoatl, whom the Aztecs expected to return to establish his kingdom.

By the reign of Moctezuma II (1502–1520), about 15 million people in central and southern Mexico paid tribute to the Aztecs.

Hernán Cortés claimed all of Mexico for the king of Spain. A Christian, he destroyed the temples and idols because they were used in rites of human sacrifice.

Cortés received Doña Marina, a captive princess who spoke several languages, as a gift. Her skill as an interpreter and her advice on Indian matters helped him conquer the Aztecs.

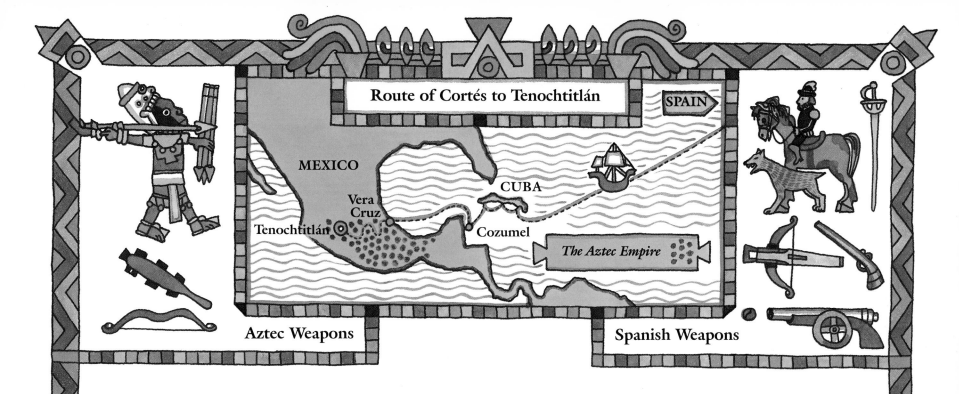

Route of Cortés to Tenochtitlán

SPAIN

MEXICO

Vera Cruz

CUBA

Tenochtitlán

Cozumel

The Aztec Empire

Aztec Weapons

Spanish Weapons

Cortés came to Mexico against the orders of his Spanish commander, who had decided someone else should lead this important expedition. By burning his ships, Cortés committed himself and his forces to a successful invasion, since there was now no escape.

Cortés entered Tenochtitlán in 1519 with 400 men. He returned in 1521 with 900 Spanish soldiers and thousands of Indian allies.

In early battles Aztec warriors fought until they had conquered their opponents, but in later wars both sides fought only until an agreed-upon number of prisoners had been taken alive. Aztecs believed that the sun's spirit needed human blood for strength to return from the underworld each dawn, and they took prisoners to offer as sacrificial victims.

Cortés won Mexico for Spain by means of brilliant tactics and superior weapons. Clubs with obsidian (lava glass) blades, bows and arrows, and spears launched from hand-held wooden throwers called atlatls were no match for Spanish cannons, steel swords, muskets, crossbows, guns, horses, attack dogs, and, finally, ships.

Moctezuma's nephew Cuauhtemoc (Kwow-TEM-ok) succeeded him as emperor. Cuauhtemoc was captured and hanged by Cortés.

Moctezuma's body was thrown into the lake. Cortés' remains lie in Mexico City.

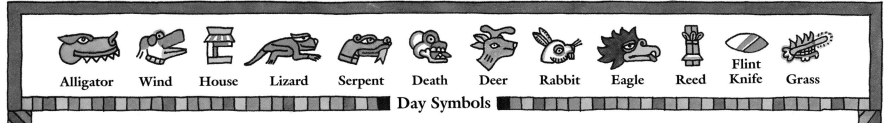

The Aztecs used several calendar systems: a 260-day sacred calendar, a 365-day solar calendar, and a 52-year calendar "bundle."

The sacred calendar was divided into 13 cycles of 20 days. The 20 different names for the days rotated until the calendar returned to the starting point, "one alligator." A child born on a particular day received that day's name and cycle number and might be called 2-deer, 5-lizard, 9-alligator, 13-reed.

Just as there was a name and number for each day, each year was given a number from 1 to 13 and one of the names of four sacred calendar days: reed, flint knife, house, or rabbit.

At the end of a 52-year bundle, or era, the priests would hold a New Fire Ceremony. If the gods were pleased, the universe would continue, and the solar and secular calendars began again.

Quetzalcoatl's return was predicted for the year 1-Reed, which would occur only once in a bundle. The last known New Fire Ceremony was held in our year 1507 (2-Reed). If you count each subsequent year down and toward the right on this page, you will see that the year 1-Reed was 1519 on our calendar—the year Cortés arrived in Mexico.

Much of what we know about Aztec calendars is recorded on the famous twelve-ton stone calendar disk in a museum in Mexico City. Other sources of Aztec symbols are the fold-out books called codices. Because the Spaniards destroyed almost all the books they found, no pre-1519 Aztec codex still exists.

Year Signs

New Fire Symbol (Always 2-Reed)

Aztec Calendar

Mexican Codex